CURSIVE HANDWRITING
workbook for kids

EMAIL US AT

modernkidpress@gmail.com

TO GET FREE GOODIES!

_____

Just title the email "Free Goodies Please!"

And we will send some extra

surprises your way!

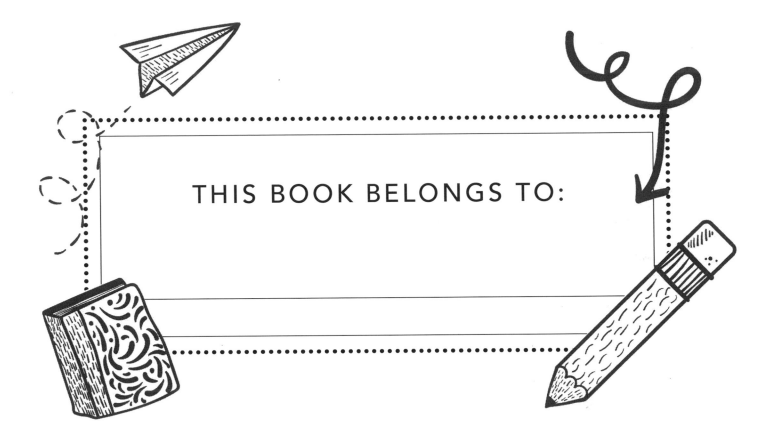

THIS BOOK BELONGS TO:

WHY TEACH YOUR CHILDREN CURSIVE?

We believe it is still so important to teach your children the art and skill of cursive handwriting. Even in this digital age, putting pen to paper is known to stimulate the brain more than anything else. Here are just a few of the benefits:

1. As children grow into adults they will need to sign their name on all sorts of important documents. Cursive helps them develop a unique signature. Research has shown that cursive signatures are harder to forge than print.

2. Research has suggested that writing cursive letters activates a different part of the brain than printing letters. Learning cursive is also good for practicing fine motor skills.

3. The physical act of writing in cursive leads to a higher level of comprehension. Additionally, writing in cursive is generally faster than writing in print, so as children get older it can be more efficient, especially in test taking scenarios.

a a a a

a

a a a a

August _August_

ant _ant_

apple _apple_

always _always_

B B B B

b

b *b* *b* *b*

Betsy *Betsy*

bike *bike*

bird *bird*

bear *bear*

C C C C

C

C   C   C   C

Carol Carol

car car

color color

cat cat

Denver Denver

dive dive

donut donut

deer deer

d

d d d d

D

D D D D

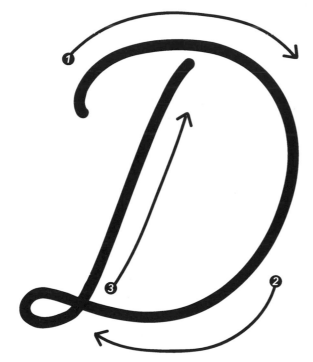

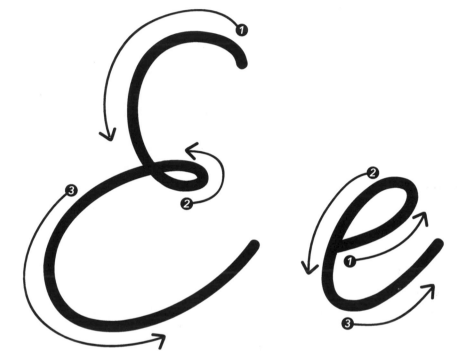

E E E E

e

e e e e

Europe *Europe*

elbow *elbow*

eat *eat*

elf *elf*

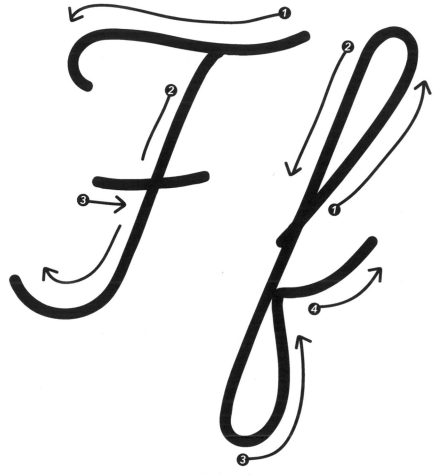

$\mathcal{F}\ \mathcal{F}\ \mathcal{F}\ \mathcal{F}$

f

Friday Friday

fruit fruit

fly fly

fox fox

g

g *g* *g* *g*

Greta Greta

give give

got got

green green

H h

$\mathcal{H}$ $\mathcal{H}$ $\mathcal{H}$ $\mathcal{H}$ $\mathcal{H}$

h

h *h* *h* *h*

Henry Henry

have have

hat hat

hear hear

l *l* *l* *l*

i

i i i i

Illinois *Illinois*

ice *ice*

in *in*

ivy *ivy*

J J J J

j

j *j* *j* *j*

Jack Jack

jump jump

joy joy

jet jet

K k

K K K K K

k

k k k k

Kate Kate

key key

kid kid

kite kite

L

L L L L

ℓ *ℓ* *ℓ* *ℓ* *ℓ*

Luke Luke

lid lid

lake lake

leaf leaf

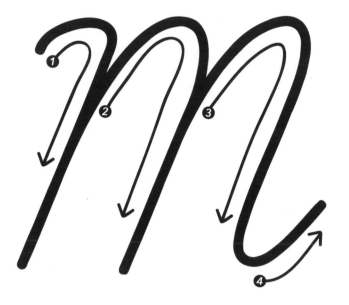

mmmm

m

m m m m

May May

man man

map map

milk milk

n *n* *n* *n*

n

n *n* *n* *n*

Nate Nate

nut nut

nine nine

neck neck

O

𝒪 𝒪 𝒪 𝒪

o

O O O O

Ohio Ohio

oak oak

one one

owl owl

p *p* *p* *p*

p

p p p p

Peter Peter

pig pig

pet pet

plant plant

Q

Q Q Q Q

q

q q q q

Quinn Quinn

queen queen

quiz quiz

quote quote

R R R R

r

Ruby Ruby

rock rock

roll roll

read read

S

S

𝓘 𝓘 𝓘 𝓘

Saturn *Saturn*

say *say*

sail *sail*

star *star*

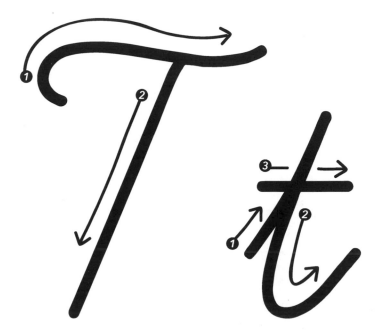

$\mathcal{T}$ $\mathcal{T}$ $\mathcal{T}$ $\mathcal{T}$ $\mathcal{T}$

t

t *t* *t* *t*

Trent Trent

tag tag

tent tent

talk talk

U U U U U

u

u u u u

Utah Utah

up up

use use

under under

V V V V V

u *u* *u* *u*

Violet *Violet*

van *van*

vase *vase*

vote *vote*

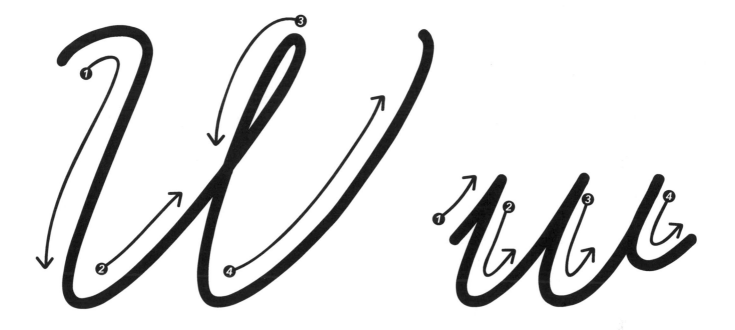

w w w w w

W

w w w w

Wendy *Wendy*

wet *wet*

week *week*

wild *wild*

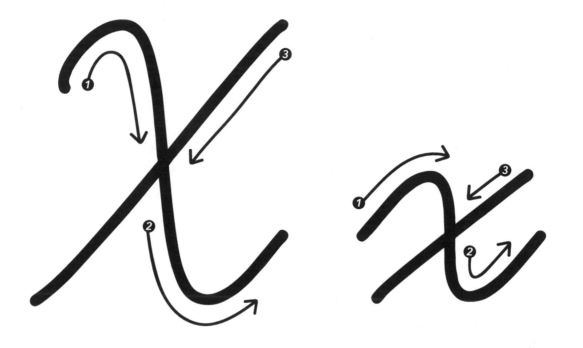

X

X X X X

x

x   x   x   x

Xavier Xavier

box box

axe axe

six six

Y Y Y Y

y

y *y* *y* *y*

Yale *Yale*

you *you*

yet *yet*

yard *yard*

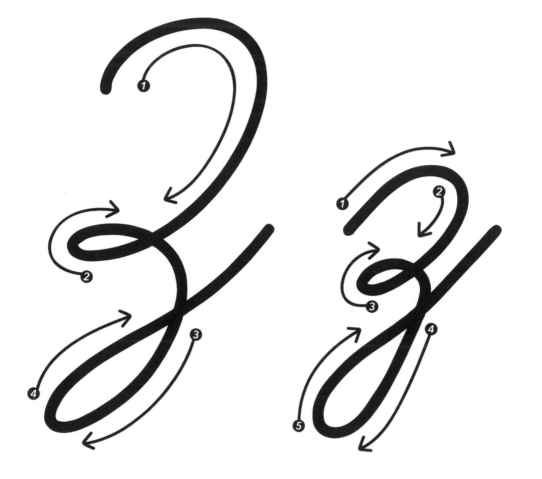

Z

𝒵 𝒵 𝒵 𝒵

Zara Zara

zip zip

zero zero

zebra zebra